SALFORD  S

by

Cliff Hayes

MEMORIES

Published by   **'Memories'**
T/A Castlefield Publications
Dawson Street
Manchester, M3 4JZ
Tel: **061 832 3917**

© **Cliff Hayes**   *Cliff Hayes*

Produced by   **Northern Publishing Services**
28 Bedford Road, Firswood
Manchester, M16 0JA
Tel: **061 862 9399**

Printed by   **Manchester Free Press**
Longford Trading Estate
Thomas Street, Stretford
Manchester, M32 0JT

> *A great deal of research has gone into this volume and it has entailed drinking asking questions in many Salford Ale Houses to ferret out the stories. The names of the pubs and the men have been changed in case I ever need to go back to those pubs again.*

ACKNOWLEDGEMENTS

Thanks to Salford Local History Library for the loan of some of the photos used in the book, and especially to Tim and Tony for their help and information. To Ted Gray, for photographs and information. To Douglas Britton, Manchester's Town Crier, for his additional knowledge and information, and to The Manchester Ship Canal Company for permission to lift from their Port of Manchester Review magazines and help with information.

INTRODUCTION

I need no apology for calling this book "Salford Docks". We all know that the official title of the Docks was "Manchester" Docks and that the Company that ran them was the "Manchester" Ship Canal Company. You can also point out that numbers 1, 2, 3 & 4 docks at Pomona were in Manchester. Well they were in Old Trafford, a district of Stretford U.D.C. The only bit of the docks that were actually inside the Manchester City boundary was the top of No. One Dock, BUT the real heart of the docks were in Salford! The main docks numbered 6, 7, 8, & 9, and the largest area of the docks were inside the Salford boundary AND even more important the men who worked on the docks, the thousands of men who sweated and heaved the cargoes off the vessels after they had made the 28 mile journey from the Mersey Estuary, and who seemed sometimes almost like an army of ants in those labour intensive days; those men in the main were SALFORD men, (Ordsall men, Eccles men, Seedley men) and what did they call the place where they worked...

SALFORD DOCKS

ABOUT THE AUTHOR

Cliff Hayes, editor, author, publisher and broadcaster are all titles that can be attributed to this ebullient character. He came to Manchester over twenty years ago after marrying a local girl and getting a job with the newspapers at Thompson House in Manchester. Before that he had spent seven years at sea working as a Ship's Printer which took him all over the world. His travels gave him a unique insight into the workings of the great ports throughout the world. His great interest and love of local history has led him to both publishing and broadcasting, and his ideals of bringing to the general public, publications that are both interesting and factual, breathes life into our history to enable us to see and appreciate what is around us, thus enriching our lives now and in the future.

Cliff's collection of facts and pictures brings to you the story of Salford Docks, that were 40 miles from the open sea! A permanent reminder of what men can achieve with the will and foresight and strength of character that still prevails today. The great Dockland area is undergoing a metamorphosis that, for anyone who was involved there when it was a working docks, is astounding, as we head for the 21st century.

BEFORE THE DOCKS

Salford Docks came about because of the need for somewhere to unload the ocean-going vessels once they had been enticed up the Mersey and into the newly built Manchester Ship Canal. Looking at the maps on page 5 of this book, you can see that the area was an automatic choice really, as it was the biggest open space nearest to Manchester that they could get. The Earl of Tatton owned most of the land from New Barns to the River Irwell. It wasn't the best of land, being damp and somewhat boggy, so the site of the large docks was obvious. The Bridgewater Canal Company had been bought during the lead up to the construction of the Ship Canal so the land from Throstle Mill to Cornbrook came with that Company and so was ideal to build the 4 smaller docks (Pomona). Note particularly the bend in the river marked Maud Wheel, later Mode Wheel Locks; the straightening out of which gave the Trafford family more land and gave the Ship Canal Company a toe-hold in Trafford Park.

There has been a lot written on the Manchester Ship Canal itself, and undoubtedly, Ted Gray's book "Manchester Ship Canal - 100 years" is one of the best, and therefore there is no need to cover any of that ground again. This volume will concentrate on the docks themselves and the men who worked on them; their lives and their working conditions.

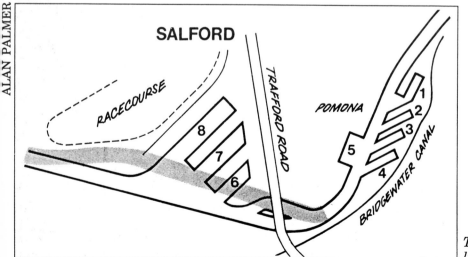

The building of the Docks caused disruption to the normally placid Irwell. A public meeting in Ordsall on the 25th July 1893 had the Mayor, and officials listening to complaints of smells, disease and debris all coming from Salford Docks. The Town Council initiated an enquiry.

ALAN PALMER

The Docks as planned in 1885. The shaded line was the original River Irwell.

A 1950 photo taken by Ted Gray captures the bustle of the docks.

SALFORD BEFORE THE DOCKS

Features worth looking for and studying are the Roman Road (now Chester Road); The Blind Asylum (now the site of Police Headquarters); Ordsall Hall (still there and well worth visiting); Eccles New Road, the Railway and Cross Lane Station, at the top and the oddly marked Campfield which became Salford Borough Cemetery. Some books tell you that the Botanical Gardens at Old Trafford were cleared to build the docks at Pomona but as you can see they were the other side of Chester Road. They were gardens at Pomona (Cornbrook) but there had gone before the Docks came along.

RIVER CRUISES

Mention must also be made of Stan Salt and his lovely boat the 'Princess Katherine'. Stan's cruises and trips on the Irwell and the Manchester Ship Canal help to keep the docks alive. It's always a pleasure when walking around the area to see Stan pass with another boat full of happy trippers sharing in Stan's vast knowledge of the docks. To join Captain Salt call 061 - 736 2108.

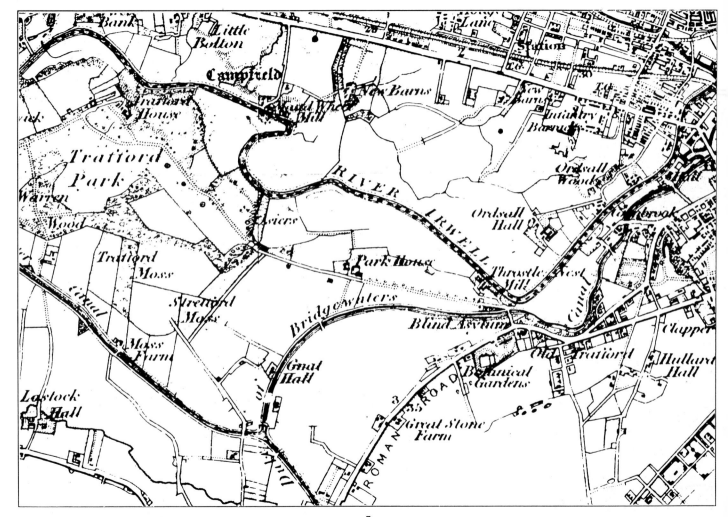

MANCHESTER DOCKS.

The Dock Estate covers an area of 700 acres, of which 179 acres is water space. Quays are 5¼ miles in length. The height of the quay wall is about 8 feet above ordinary water level.

The Dimensions of the Docks, etc., are :—

No. 1	..	780 by 120 feet	No. 6	..	850 by 225 feet.
„ 2	..	600 by 150 „	„ 7	..	1,160 by 225 „
„ 3	..	600 by 150 „	„ 8	..	1,340 by 250 „
„ 4	..	560 by 150 „	„ 9	..	2,700 by 200 „

Trafford Wharf—Length, 1,653 feet.
Salford Quay—Length, 1,100 feet.

The Manchester Ship Canal Company built the docks at Salford, and they, by and large, hired and fired and paid the men who worked there. They were completely independent from other dockyards in the country. They had their own police force; their own private railway lines and the locomotives to run it; they had their own fire service and the 'Firefly' a fire ship to put out fires.

The docks opened on January 1st 1894 and about 900 men were employed that day to start unloading the vessels coming up the Canal. The police force, a body of 16 men (1 Superintendent and 15 Constables) had been sworn in only days before on Christmas Day and 'Pioneer' a ship owned by the Co-operative movement was the first to start unloading. There were only 7 docks to start with 1-4 and 6-8. Number 5 dock which was planned to be off Ordsall Road and facing Ordsall Hall was never cut and number 9 dock came along later when they had got rid of the Race Course, which again was known as Manchester Races though it was in Salford. The map opposite shows the docks in 1908 and rewards a closer study. The open area opposite Pomona and next to Tatton Mills (bottom right) is where number 5 dock was to be built, and note the railway under Trafford Road and under Ordsall (alongside Ellesmere Street).

THE CARGOES

Cotton was one reason the ship canal was built, raw cotton being its main import. As the docks grew busier, grain, oats, wheat etc., and other cargoes grew in importance. Timber unloaded at Barton and Trafford Wharf was left to weather in large timber yards. Other cargoes were Lamp Black or Carbon Black and coal (disliked by the men because they were so dirty). There were no showers in those days and the men went home black! Many local pubs had a sign on the bar Parlour or Snug "No Lamp Black" to keep out workers who may dirty the furniture. Local industry soon found an outlet through the docks to export their goods, even steam engines and carriages were shipped all over the world from Salford.

Just to set the record straight it used to take about a week to turn a small to medium-sized freight ship around - that is unload, store away, and reload the ship. It was the same in Liverpool, Bristol or London about one or two weeks. Salford tried, and succeeded to turn the ship around faster so that the six or seven hours each way on the canal was compensated by faster unloading. If you sailed into Liverpool on the Friday it was the next Friday or even the following Monday before you could be away with your next cargo. Sail up the Ship Canal on a Friday and the company got you unloaded and your next cargo on board and down the Canal by the next Friday.

So coming to Salford did not lose you time. The rates were cheaper, so the cost of travelling up the Canal (£100 in 1894) were offset by the lower charges for the unloading etc., and your goods were much further inland, saving transport costs.

It was not until containers came along that all the finely balanced equations were upset. Out of seven days in port, one a half were spent traversing the Canal (about 10%) and that time was made up by speed of turn-round. When containers had established themselves the unloading and loading was reduced to a day or a day and a half, so instead of being able to absorb and match the turn-round time, Salford was now taking twice as long; this was the start of the demise of the docks.

The docks, by the late 1970s had all but finished and as Manchester Liners had left in 1979, by the early 1980s there were only scrap boats and the odd ship in the docks.

The first sign of the containerisation was in the late 1960s when Middle East freight came in sealed pallets. Before that everything had to be handled on to pallets from the hold and the pallets winched ashore and handled onto the lorries or trucks and stored in the warehouses until ready to be claimed or forwarded. There would be 6 or 8 men per gang, and two to four gangs on a ship, all very labour intensive.

Bales of cotton being unloaded in the 1920s. Three bales at a time and 4 men complete with dockers' hooks to pull them ashore.

The Guinness Boats were a regular feature of Pomona Docks with their runs from Dublin. 'The Lady Grania' and her sister ship 'The Lady Gwendolen', were named after ladies in the Guinness family. This traffic, which Arthur Guinness started in about 1900 still comes into the canal but, from the early 1970s, only as far as Weston Point, Runcorn and in bulk containers.

This picture from 1934 shows Australian lamb being unloaded straight on to wagons for same-day forward shipment. The first frozen meat came into Salford Docks in the 1920s though there had been refrigerated and cooled ships before that.

I was told a story from 1938 of an accident on the docks and an ambulance was called for. As the two injured lads were being settled in the ambulance, two stretcher-bearers came round the corner with another injury and jumping straight in the vehicle, advised immediate movement as the victim was very cold. The ambulance took off, but once through the Dock Gates the attendants informed the driver that a miraculous recovery had taken place and when he pulled up, they jumped out, complete with the whole frozen lamb which had been on the stretcher.

Everything had to be lifted and man-handled, every crate needed two men to lift it on to the hoist, unload, store away or put onto the wagons. Some cargoes would be handled six times before leaving the docks. Here crates of fruit head for Manchester's Wholesale Fruit and Vegetable Market c.1938

> *Compared with other major engineering feats, there was quite a loss of life in the building of the Ship Canal. From January 1st, 1888 to October 1893 when the canal was almost complete 154 men were killed whilst working on it, and 186 permanently injured. Though how many accidents happened at the Salford end is unknown. There were 1,404 men temporarily disabled in minor accidents.*

Men unloading the first cargo of citrus fruits from South Africa. Lemons, grapefruit, Cape oranges and limes, in 1934. The ship was the SS 'Banffshire' owned by Turnbull, Martin and Co., and had picked up its cargo on the Manchester-Australia/New Zealand service (all foodstuffs).

I found this poem written by Ian Mackinnon in an old back number of Port of Manchester Review, Ian was, or is, a pilot with the Manchester Ship Canal Co., I hope he will not mind me reprinting the first two verses of his poem. . .

AN INTERVIEW

A local historian you say,
And for my memories you'll pay!
Then I suggest, without delay,
to the Salisbury we repair, where
at the bar, over a jar
talk of docks, ships and jolly Jack Tars.

In there lads, grab that pew
For History's sake we'll sup a few.
Two pints of best, round's on you.
Now, to bring the past nearer,
close your eyes to hear clearer
voices from a bygone era.

"Three bitters and a mild, Lil,
and none of yer blinkin' swill"

Ian Mackinnon.

The bananas were picked green and were unloaded still green. They were hung in a ripening room at Fyffes' Warehouse and did not leave the docks before they were ripe.

The Salford City Reporter in 1948 had a letter asking for recipes using green bananas. One West Indian lady living locally answered with 'Green Banana Stew' which was printed in the paper. A week later a representative from Fyffes appeared in front of the editor asking who wrote the original inquiry as green bananas were not allowed out of the docks until they had ripened and not to repeat the recipe as the green bananas were going missing at an alarming rate.

Taken from the Salford Reporter of Saturday July 22nd 1893

"There will be an inquest as to whether Manchester or Salford will have the honour of building the Foreign Animal Receiving House that will service the new docks. A Board of Agriculture inspector, the Hon. Thomas Henry W. Pelham, Barrister will sit in judgement as the Town Clerks of Manchester and Salford will state their cases."

This was unusual and seemed to be collusion, as both Town Clerks were quoted as saying that they were not paying big sums to lawyers to mystify the Inspectors. It seems to be the only case I can find where the two Town Clerks had got together previously and decided to battle it out face to face. Manchester and Salford fought a long battle but Manchester won and the pens were on Trafford Wharf just opposite Mode Wheel.

Turkeys and chickens for Christmas 1952, all the way from Australia. They were frozen or tinned.

Salford Docks has seen many unusual cargoes. Steam trains and coaches often passed through on their way to far flung corners of the Empire, but 1975 saw one of the few that returned. (Below) David Shepherd saved a steam engine in Zambia and returned it to this country via Salford Docks and it now steams on the East Somerset Railway.

A 30 ton load of machinery goes aboard the 'Manchester Merchant'. c.1950.

Worth studying in this picture is the Railway which ran under Ordsall and was built on the 'Cut and Cover' principle. Quite a few houses in Ordsall were demolished to make way for the line which ran under Trafford Road and through the area to link up at Windsor Bridge with the L & Y Main line. There was a station at New Barns which served the Racecourse for many years, becoming a parcel depot for the Ship Canal when the races moved to Castle Irwell,. Worth noting also is the number of houses on the far side of Trafford Road.

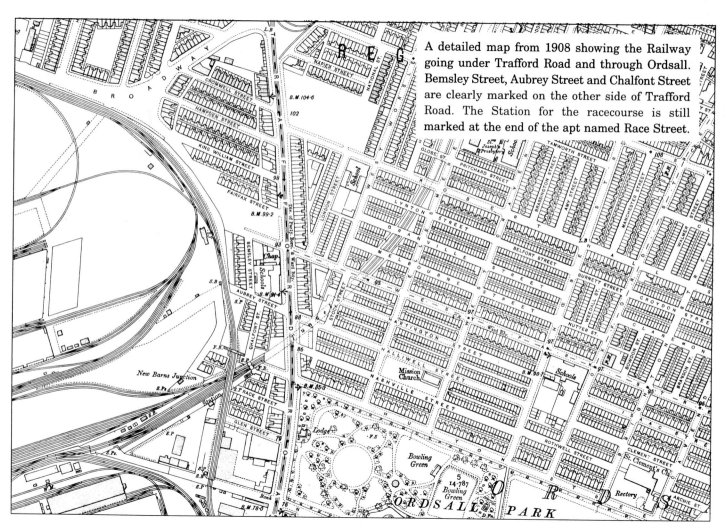

A detailed map from 1908 showing the Railway going under Trafford Road and through Ordsall. Bemsley Street, Aubrey Street and Chalfont Street are clearly marked on the other side of Trafford Road. The Station for the racecourse is still marked at the end of the apt named Race Street.

The full aerial photograph of Salford Docks c.1950.

The Docks have always been exciting and full of life none more so than when they hosted 'Open Day'. Here in June 1924, Destroyers and naval war ships came up to Salford to mark the birthday of the then Prince of Wales.

A panoramic view of the docks from a 1920s expanding post card from A. Bown of 143 Trafford Road, Salford. The Dry Docks are marked and Mode Wheel Locks can be made out. The Grain Elevator (No. 1) caught fire when bombed in the second world war and burned for nearly 6 months on and off. Note the vast amount of sidings on page 26 and the wood left to 'season'.

As mentioned before, Salford Docks had its own private railway. The Manchester Ship Canal Railway - the largest private railway in the country.

Here a loco pulls wagons across the rail swing bridge from Salford Docks to Trafford Wharf. Locos, 'New York' 'Bombay' and 'New Orleans' also in the picture. Salford Quays Cinema block is now where the hoarding (top right) was then.

A Ship Canal Steam loco pulling wagons across the Trafford Warf Rail Bridge

Where there was work, there were workers, and among the workers were poor conditions, and among the poor and bad conditions were the preachers and the missionaries.

Here from around a century ago, the Manchester City Mission, read a gospel and sing-a-long from the steps of their Higson Caravan around the Salford Docks.

Thousands of tons of wheat, oats and barley came in every week from Canada and Australia. Floating grain barges took it to the elevators for storage but some went straight into the Bridgewater barges and down the canal to Kellogg's in Trafford Park. The last load of maize was delivered to Kelloggs on 29th March 1974. Between 1938 and 1974 over 3,000,000 tons was delivered to the factory without one lorry involved.

Butter in crates arriving from Australia in 1952. Note the bales of straw as a crude loading stage for the refrigerated lorry waiting, doors open, to be loaded. Every man in the picture has a flat cap on!

Men queuing for wages at Salford Docks - July 1897

When the first men were employed on January 1st 1894 the Company were worried that un-trained local men would not know enough about unloading or dock work in general. So as well as the three hundred local men that had been employed, men were sent from Glasgow, Liverpool and Barrow-in-Furness, often recruited surreptitiously, to train these men. Within a month the locals thought they could do the job without these 'strangers' and an agitation was started on the Monday morning outside the Dock Gates with hundreds of local unemployed men from Manchester and Salford. Over 1,500 men gathered outside the Dock Gates and from here they marched to Salford Town Hall where they met with Ship Canal Company representatives. Finally they agreed to disperse on the understanding that 300 of them would be taken on the next morning. This was done, but many of the 'strangers' from Liverpool, Glasgow and Barrow never went home and settled in the area.

After small profits in the 1970s, 1980 saw the Docks lose £3 million and in 1981 that loss climbed to £4 million. Too many ports competed for a dwindling shipping market. The fall off of goods from the Commonwealth, and more goods from the E.E.C., which naturally used the East Coast ports which are so much nearer, accelerated the decline.

Manchester Liners played a great part in the rise and success of the Salford Docks. Formed in 1898 by Christopher Furness of the Furness Withy Company along with other shippers from the North East. They won a contract for bringing in Indian cotton and exporting finished goods.

Sunday Morning, and the sailors from visiting warships head for church to join locals in their religious service.

The Docks played a large part in Britain's War Effort in both the First and Second World War.

Above is a picture of American troops and their supplies being unloaded on to horse-drawn carts in 1918. During the Second World War the higher reaches of the Ship Canal and quieter corners of the Docks were used to store captured enemy vessels. Some German merchant vessels were captured coming across the Atlantic and were moored near Barton while their fate was decided. They were stripped of their stores which were piled on the quay-side. Next morning the stores had vanished and the police were telling of local children running through the streets carrying tins and packets with their contents and instructions in German. "What's for tea Mum?", "Open and see!"

The Grain Elevator (No. 2) that stood at the head of No.9 dock, built after the first World War. The photo shows the extent of the railway sidings between No.8 and 9 docks and the closeness of the houses behind.

The extent to which the cargoes had to be man-handled can be demonstrated in the above picture, which shows cargoes coming together ready for export, and imports being stored before inland delivery. All sacks, bales etc had to be lifted and placed by hand as the only mechanisation was a hoist and a trolley. This is the new transit shed on No. 7 dock, pictured just after opening, with road and rail access for undercover loading and unloading.

Hundreds of people worked on Salford Docks, and a good transport service was needed to get them to and from work. Trafford Road had its own Dock Terminus where the No. 70 & 71 routes turned round. Here trams 235 & 291 are caught getting ready to head off. The No. 70 is on the circular route which included Broughton Lane and the No. 71 in the anti-clockwise direction via Manchester.

Salford Docks had its own private police force that started with 16 men in 1893 and grew to about 100 by the 1950s. There were 25 dock police in 1993 when the security was handed over to an outside private firm. The high walls around the Docks were also dismantled.

There was one murder, the Dock Police had to deal with. This took place on April 1st 1944 on board M.V. 'Pacific Shipper', which had just crossed the Atlantic in a war-time convoy. The crew were paid off and the radio officer, a James William Percey, stayed on board. A week later a strange smell was noticed coming from his cabin and on breaking in, he was found murdered. An axe was found in another cabin and James Galbraith was arrested, and though he pleaded not guilty, he was convicted and hung on April 26th the same year - all over within a month!

The discipline in the Dock Police Force was very strict. In the early years many men did not last long and those getting a job were told to move away from Ordsall and keep themselves apart from the men they watched over. Before the First World War many police were disciplined themselves for drinking on duty or reporting for duty drunk.

The Police watched for everything even slipping off for a 'smoke' and issued an impressive document called a misconduct form (nick-named a 'Split Sheet') if you were caught..

There is no way to disguise the fact that a lot of goods went missing from the docks. There are many, sometimes amusing stories of things vanishing from Salford Docks, and stories of dock workers dropping one case out of every load, just to check what was inside, takes some believing.

Although there was some very heavy and organised crime, much of the stealing was 'chancers' just one-offs, when men were tempted by goods lying around. Many dockers were caught, and were always dismissed on the spot. Not everyone was on the 'knock' and there were many honest hard-working dockers, usually prompted by the little woman at home. The fear of losing their job was a great deterrent, and they could probably buy stolen goods in the pub later at less risk.

A lot of goods were recovered, as in 1978 when £46,000 worth of goods went missing, but £33,000 worth were recovered. The worst year for theft was 1975 when £67,500 worth of goods went walking, £29,000 worth was recovered.

The Salford Docks did not die suddenly. Their life was chipped away as company after company decided that money spoke louder than the jobs and the needs of the workforce at the top end of the Canal. If the ships and the work were not there, then the need for workers diminished. The numbers of dockers employed by the Ship Canal tell the story:-

1970	c.1,500
1975	826
1980	654
1984	the closure announced
1985	26

Manchester Liners tried very hard to keep the docks open. They invested heavily in containers in the early 1970s but it became increasingly difficult to justify the extra costs. Also the docks went through a difficult time with the union/management relationship which deteriorated on both sides.

Number 9 dock under construction before it opened in 1905.

One of the notable events during the year has been the slow demolition of No 2 Grain Elevator. Built in the 1920s it was one of the first reinforced concrete structures in the country and had a capacity of 40,000 tons, with 260 storage bins and 81 transit bins. The weight of the building and machinery was 160,000 tons and it stood 168 ft high, being 295 ft long and 165 ft wide. A model of No 2 Granary was exhibited at the British Empire Exhibition, Wembley 1924-25.

  For almost 60 years this fine building stood impressively at the head of No 9 dock and she has only given up her position very reluctantly.

We all remember the reluctant demolition of the grain elevator. They had to blow it with dynamite several times before it finally collapsed.

No.8 dock and look how close Salford and the pub on Trafford Road is to the Bittern (British and Continental SS Co.) just in from Rotterdam emphasising the problem of policing the docks.

The second 'Firefly', delivered July 1935 as a fire and salvage tug. Pictured here in January 1936. During the second World War it was this vessel and her crew that kept down the bomb damage on the docks.

Another unuasal vessel always to be found at the docks was th 60-ton floating crane - pictured here in No7 dock in 1971.

Submarines at Trafford Wharf. - October 1963

The Docks provided a lot of work, not just for the dockers and clerical workers, but for firms such as these who provided services.

Agents, Forwarders, Repair Yards and Fitters were all involved
and depended for their livelihoods on Salford Docks.

47

SALFORD LOCAL HISTORY LIBRARY

Peel Park, Salford, M5 4WU. Tel: 061 736 2649

If you are interested in tracing your ancestors or learning more about the area in which you live, we've got a lot to offer you. You can research your family tree, or see how your neighbourhood has changed over the years. At **Salford Local History Library** on the Crescent you'll find maps, street directories, photographs, postcards and a whole range of things to get you started.

OPENING HOURS: LIBRARY
10:00am to 5:00pm on
Monday, Tuesday, Thursday and Friday;
10:00 to 9:00pm on Wednesday;
Closed on Saturday and Sunday.

(Car park, disabled access and café.)

STAFF:
Tim Ashworth (Local History Librarian),
Tony Frankland (Assistant Local History Librarian),
Sandra Hayton (Library Assistant),
Patricia Nutall (Library Assistant).